Managing Your Emotions

Keeping Your Feelings from
Running the Show

Amy Baker

New
Growth
Press

www.newgrowthpress.com

New Growth Press, Greensboro, NC 27404
www.newgrowthpress.com
Copyright © 2013 by Amy Baker

All Scripture quotations, unless otherwise indicated, are taken from the *Holy Bible,* New International Version®, NIV®. Copyright © 1973, 1978, 1984 by International Bible Society. Used by permission of Zondervan. All rights reserved.

Scripture quotations marked The Message are taken from *The Message.* Copyright © 1993, 1994, 1995, 1996, 2000, 2001, 2002. Used by permission of NavPress Publishing Group.

Cover Design: Faceout books, faceout.com
Typesetting: Lisa Parnell, lparnell.com

ISBN-10: 1-939946-41-7
ISBN-13: 978-1-939946-41-6

Library of Congress Cataloging-in-Publication Data
Baker, Amy, 1959–
  Managing your emotions : keeping your feelings from running the show / Amy Baker.
      pages cm
  Includes bibliographical references and index.
  ISBN 978-1-939946-41-6 (alk. paper)
  1. Emotions—Religious aspects—Christianity. 2. Psychology, Religious. I. Title.
  BV4597.3.B345 2013
  248.4—dc23   2013020292

Printed in Canada

20 19 18 17 16 15 14 13   1 2 3 4 5

Yesterday, I started thinking about what my brother did to me when I was eight. All the old feelings of shame came flooding back, and I couldn't focus on anything else. ~Ali

I missed class three times last week after my boyfriend and I broke up. I feel so depressed. All I want to do is sleep and try to forget about how bad I feel. Nothing has ever hurt so much in my life. ~Kaitlin

That stupid driver just cut me off. Who does he think he is? I feel like teaching him a lesson. ~Jasmine

No one talked to me at church on Sunday. I feel like an outsider. ~Donna

My four-year-old threw a tantrum in the middle of the grocery store today. I was so embarrassed. I feel like I'm a failure as a parent. ~Kathy

My professor wants me to revise my thesis. I've spent hundreds of hours on it. I feel like quitting. ~Mei

Feelings, or emotions, are a powerful part of our lives. So powerful, in fact, that they can control our very being. Have you ever been overwhelmed by shame? Exhausted by depression? Consumed with anger? Dominated by rejection? Devoured by bitterness? Most of us can say yes to at least a few of those negative emotions. But do we have to be controlled by our emotions?

There is a better way to live than being constantly in the grip of your emotions. You don't have to be trapped by negative emotions and let them run your life. Instead of being dominated by your emotions, you can learn to understand them, turn to God for help and hope, and even make your emotions work for you instead of against you. It starts by understanding how God made you and your emotions.

Emotions Are Part of God's Good Creation

God intended for emotions to be a good part of our makeup. After creating Adam (with emotions), God looked at what he had created with great satisfaction and proclaimed his creation of Adam, "very good" (Genesis 1:31). Feelings are a good part of who we are created to be. God created us in his image, and God has emotions. God grieves, God rejoices, God weeps, God exults, God is angry, and God loves.[1] Because we are made in his image, we too experience emotions.

Emotions enable us to laugh, to rejoice, and to enjoy. Emotions allow us to experience affection, love, passion, and ardor. Emotions allow us to be glad, to delight, to know elation, and to be passionate. Emotions are a good part of God's creation.

Surprisingly, we could also argue that the capacity to experience "negative" emotions was also part of God's good creation. Because it can be difficult to see value in negative emotions, we might conclude that all negative emotions—sadness, loneliness, frustration, fear—are the consequences of sin. However, when no suitable helper was found for Adam and God declared it was not good for man to be alone, we can probably safely assume some negative emotion was attached to this evaluation—perhaps sadness, loneliness, or frustration. But sadness didn't turn to depression, loneliness didn't turn to despair, frustration didn't turn to rage. At that time living in a perfect garden untouched by sin, a perfect remedy was immediately presented. God created Eve, and when God brought her to Adam, Adam emotionally responded, "Wow, she's like me!" Although God's Word doesn't tell us for sure, we can probably safely infer that Adam's delight was enhanced because he experienced negative emotions earlier when no suitable helper was found. Prior to the fall it seems reasonable that "negative" emotions were simply the catalyst that produced more brilliant positive emotions

Broken by Sin

Sadly, when sin entered the world, every aspect of humanity was affected, including our feelings. Rather than being the catalyst leading to heightened positive feelings, negative emotions now produced misery and despair. Feelings became twisted and warped. Prior to Adam and Eve's fall into sin, there was always a perfect remedy for bad emotions. Before the fall, Adam and Eve knew nothing of shame, grief, depression, anger, fear, and discouragement as we experience them today. Prior to the fall, emotions were never instruments of sin or the results of sin. Prior to the fall, Adam was never tempted to be exasperated with Eve. Prior to the fall Eve never felt hurt by Adam blaming her for his problems. Prior to the fall there were no miserable feelings resulting from sin.

Adam and Eve's world was untouched by the lousy emotions we live with every day. Today we are often plagued with feelings we wish we didn't have. We experience distress, pain, and a host of other crummy feelings with such intensity that it is tempting to wish that we didn't have the capacity to feel. It sometimes seems like it would be worth going through life numb and devoid of emotions, good or bad, in order not to experience the wretchedness bad emotions produce.

Trapped by Your Emotions

One of the ways in which sin has affected us is that our emotions easily take over and control us. Without realizing it, we can begin to make decisions based on our feelings. If it feels good, we do it. If it feels bad, we don't do it. Our emotions become the criterion by which we make everyday decisions. So Ali feels shame and focuses on her past. Kaitlin feels depressed and quits going to class. Jasmine feels angry and tailgates the driver who cut her off. Donna feels rejected and isolates herself so she won't be hurt. Kathy concludes she is a failure as a parent. Mei quits. In each case, feelings control the decision.

Dwelling on shame, sleeping through class, tailgating the driver who cut you off, isolating yourself, giving in to discouragement, and quitting aren't the solutions to bad feelings. Although letting your emotions take over seems as if it will make you feel better, it doesn't. In fact, it does just the opposite; you end up feeling worse than ever.

Being in the grip of shame, rage, fear, greed, lust, failure, self-indulgence or any other emotion feels lousy. Not only that, other bad feelings come to the party. We may experience a sense of helplessness and hopelessness. We may feel controlled and dominated, isolated or set apart from others, overwhelmed and crushed, exhausted or consumed, incapacitated and immobilized. We may feel as if we are about to fall and live with a sense of dread.

All that still doesn't make emotions bad. Remember, our Maker designed us with feelings. Emotions are still part of his good design. God wants to help us with our negative emotions. Not only that, God will do so much more for us than simply getting rid of our troubling feelings. He wants to give us a life where we are free to love him and others, free to live with purpose and significance despite how we feel at any given moment, free to step back from our feelings and depend on him for guidance.

But to live like this, we need help from outside ourselves. You already know how hard it is to change how you feel when you are angry, despairing, jealous, discouraged, and hopeless. Jesus knows that as well. He lived in our broken world where things can and did go wrong. He experienced the shame of the cross, the discouragement of being deserted by family and friends, the frustration of seeing his own people not follow God, and the grief of seeing close friends die. As Sinclair Ferguson noted,

> *He wept and groaned; he tasted human weakness and fear.* ('Never man feared like this man,' said Martin Luther of our Lord Jesus' loud crying and tears in the Garden of Gethsemane.). *He was bewildered* by what God was doing in his life ('My God, *why* have you forsaken me?' Matt. 27:46). His sympathy is not merely verbal, therefore, or

theoretical. It is actual, and real. For he is indeed our Brother, Savior, our Kinsman Redeemer.[2]

He knows emotions because he is the God who is with us. Thankfully, Jesus is also our perfect remedy. Through his perfect life and death as our substitute, we can be rescued from sin and given an alternative to being mastered by feelings. He is able to restore and make all things new—and that includes our emotions and how we respond to them.

Christ wants to reshape our emotions to reflect his and to prompt us toward faithful, kingdom-oriented living. Instead of being overcome by feelings that often lead us to pursue our own selfish desires and agendas, Christ wants to capture our hearts in such a way that, regardless of how we may feel in the moment, our ultimate desire is to serve him and his kingdom. His kingdom is governed by two basic rules: to love God with all your heart, soul, mind, and strength and to love your neighbor as yourself. Our emotions often lead us to love ourselves first, but Christ our Redeemer empowers us to resist that temptation and push forward in loving God and others.

If Not Feelings, Then What?

Christ shows us what kingdom living looks like in his response to the suffering he endured prior to his death on the cross. *The Message* paraphrases it like this:

> This is the kind of life you've been invited into, the kind of life Christ lived. He suffered everything

that came his way so you would know that it could
be done, and also know how to do it, step-by-step.

He never did one thing wrong,

Not once said anything amiss.

They called him every name in the book and he
said nothing back. He suffered in silence, content
to let God set things right. He used his servant
body to carry our sins to the Cross so we could be
rid of sin, free to live the right way. His wounds
became your healing. (1 Peter 2:21–24)

Let's unpack the implications of this passage to our
emotions. I think we would all agree that suffering, in
whatever form it takes, creates incredibly painful emotions. God's Word doesn't try to hide from us the anguish
Jesus experienced as he prepared to take the penalty that
would pay the price for our sins. As he prayed in the garden
before his arrest, we're told he was deeply distressed (Mark
14:33). Jesus told his friends, "My soul is overwhelmed
with sorrow to the point of death" (Mark 14:34). Soon
after that, he was arrested, tortured, mocked, insulted,
lied about, and unjustly sentenced to death.

So what is the example Christ left for us to follow?
Do we see a man enraged by insults? Do we see a man
cowering in fear? Do we see a man doing whatever it
takes in order to be released from his suffering and
negative emotions?

The example Jesus left is radically different than
what might be expected of someone undergoing the
intensity of suffering he experienced. They called him
every name in the book and he said nothing back. He

suffered in silence, content to let God set things right. Jesus relied on his heavenly Father. This was the pattern of Jesus's ministry from the beginning.

As you may remember, right after he was baptized and before he began his public ministry, Jesus was led into the wilderness and was tempted by Satan. He went without food for forty days and nights while he was in the wilderness, and in Matthew 4:2 we see one of the biggest understatements in the Bible. "After fasting forty days and forty nights, he [Jesus] was hungry."

Some time ago Snickers ran an engaging set of commercials showing ordinary people acting like divas or grumpy celebrities. Each commercial ended with a line something like, "You're not you when you're hungry; Snickers satisfies." The point was that when we're hungry, our emotions can take over and it's not pretty.

Jesus hadn't eaten for more than a month. Jesus had to have been famished. Since our physical condition influences our emotions, if there ever was a time when allowing feelings to dictate actions would seem appropriate and excusable, this surely would have been it.

Perhaps the devil thought that in such a physically and emotionally weakened state, Christ would certainly succumb to temptation in order to satisfy his appetite, nourish himself physically, and make himself feel better. Therefore it is surprising to hear Jesus's response to Satan's temptation to turn stones into bread. Jesus answered, "It is written: 'Man does not live on bread alone, but on every word that comes from the mouth of God'" (Matthew 4:4).

Clearly Christ communicated that our standard, our

source of truth, the basis for our decision-making is to be the Word of God. We are to be guided and directed by the truth of God's Word (depending on the Holy Spirit to illuminate it and give us proper understanding as he directs our mind, will, and emotions in the paths of truth). God's Word offers a superior way to approach life. That's why Jesus didn't give in to a raging appetite. He didn't live by the emotions that are so easily aroused by physical pressures. Even at the cross, he still lived by every word that comes from the mouth of God. That's why Jesus didn't hurl insults at those who insulted him. That's why Jesus didn't make threats. He lived by truth and he'll help us live by truth too.

Jesus could live by truth because he lived in complete dependence on the Author of truth. He told his disciples that he could do nothing without his Father in heaven (John 5:19, 30). And we can do nothing without Jesus's help (John 15:5). Do you see the pattern here? Jesus clings to the Father; we cling to Jesus. This is how we have the strength to live by "every word that comes from the mouth of the God." Jesus is our helper, our example, our rock, and our fortress. When feelings seem ready to overwhelm us, we can cling to him and receive his grace to help us live like he lived.

The ability to know and live by every word that comes from the mouth of God is much more liberating than eating a Snickers bar and going back to being yourself. We can become someone different—someone different than a girl engulfed in shame; someone different than a man gripped by anger; someone different than a graduate student demoralized by a professor.

The truth that is found in Jesus has the ability to set us free: free from the domination of fear, free from bitterness, free from worry, free from the domination of shame, free from uncontrolled anger, free from depression and hopelessness.

Free to Live by the Truth

Learning to live by every word that comes from the mouth of God is not necessarily an easy task, and certainly it is not something we can do on our own! Our feelings and desires can seem overwhelmingly powerful. Our feelings can make it seem as if we'll never be free of our depression. Our feelings can make it seem as if we can never conquer controlling anger. Our feelings can make it seem as if shame is our only option.

However, we have a gracious, compassionate Savior who helps us in our weakness. He knows what it's like to have feelings that overwhelm us. Alone in the garden the night before his crucifixion, Christ experienced such agony and anguish that his sweat fell to the ground like drops of blood. Even so, Christ is our victor. He chose to please the Father amidst excruciatingly painful emotions, and as we turn to him, he becomes our strength when our feelings seek to dominate us.

When we belong to Christ, we can be freed from the curse of sin and its enslaving hopelessness. We are redeemed by Christ, and his Spirit comes to us and gives us new freedom to become like him. Ugly emotions feel powerful, but Christ's redemption allows us to begin to use negative emotions as the catalyst to turn us to him and empower us to live for him and for others even when it feels like we can't.

Ali might begin to use the shame associated with her abuse as a vulnerable eight-year-old to lead her to a better understanding of what it meant for Christ to take the shame of the world upon himself. Ali has lived for years with the shame her brother's terrible and evil actions imposed on her. Because of this, Ali can have a better understanding of just what it meant for Someone who never did any wrong to be smeared by others' sin. Just as Ali has suffered because of another's sinful choices, Christ suffered, and his suffering made it possible for us to be cleansed from shame. As Ali remembers the cross of Christ, she comes to a Savior who also felt shame—a Savior who shed his own blood so she could be cleansed and purified from the sins committed against her and the sins she committed. Shame can drive her to Jesus— the one who understands better than anyone possibly could and the one who loves her and died for her.

Rather than leaving us disgraced and fit only for the garbage heap, Christ came to make us pure and radiant, without any stain or blemish. Of course for those who have suffered from the shameful actions of others, this is not a quick or easy process. But the resurrection gives us hope—weeping doesn't last forever. For those who know Christ and come to him, joy can grow as our trust and love for him grows.[3]

Kaitlin can also use her emotions to prompt her to look to Christ. Christ too was rejected. He knows what it is like to be turned on by the people he loved. Sadly, we were the ones rejecting Christ. He was despised and rejected *by us*. That's why he was a man of sorrows and familiar with suffering (Isaiah 53:3). Because Kaitlin has tasted rejection, her devotion and love for her Savior can become deeper. And, because he did what was right in the midst of suffering, Kaitlin can seek to follow his example. By faith she can go to Christ for her comfort, and then still by faith, attend class and take notes even though she is hurting badly after the breakup with her boyfriend.

Similarly, Jasmine, Donna, Kathy, and Mei can allow their bad feelings to lead them toward Christ and, as they turn to him, they can follow his example of living by the Word of God.

Jasmine can remember Christ's mercy to her when she is caught in sin, and she can back off, leaving a safe distance between her and the driver who cut her off. Donna can remember how Jesus sought her out when she was far from him and seek to love others even when they don't take the initiative to include her. Kathy can ask for grace from Jesus and persevere in providing instruction and discipline for her children. Mei can remind herself that ultimately she is working for the Lord and continue to work hard.

Is There Any Way to Change My Feelings?

Frequently, although certainly not always, feelings are linked to our desires, our thinking, and our actions. While we can't directly control our feelings simply by telling ourselves to buck up or be happy, we can powerfully influence them by what we choose to desire, how we think, and the way we act.

For example, if Jasmine chooses to back off and leave a safe distance between her and the driver who cut her off, she will probably feel better than if she incites herself to greater anger by honking and gesturing. But backing off is not an easy thing to do when you are angry. What is easier is to allow rage to take over. To not be overtaken by rage, Jasmine will need the help of her Savior.

For Jasmine not to be mastered by her feelings in a moment of anger, she needs to ask God for help. Instead of venting her anger or acting in anger, she can turn to her Savior, admit how angry she is and ask the Spirit to help her not express her anger in wrong actions. Notice that it isn't necessarily wrong that Jasmine feels anger—after all, another driver just endangered her life! But she can go to Jesus with her anger and ask for help in her time of need. As Jasmine receives help from the Lord, she can determine to value mercy more than vengeance. During this process she will need to remind herself of the truth of God's Word, which tells her that mercy triumphs over judgment (James 2:13) and instructs her to allow God to avenge (Romans 12:19). As Jasmine asks God for help to live out of these truths, she can receive power to bless those who have treated her wrongfully, rather than cursing them (Romans 12:14).

When Jasmine chooses to turn away from her anger and toward Christ for the power to desire, think, and act in these ways, she will gradually realize that her feelings are not mastering her. In fact, she will probably find that emotions of peace and satisfaction are growing because God has been her helper and she has followed Christ's example. She has glorified God and lived as a member of God's kingdom.

There may be times when bad feelings don't seem to be linked to your desires, thoughts, or actions. On these occasions it is probably wise to ask God to help you search your heart in case wrong thoughts and desires are influencing you without your realization. You may also want to explore physical influences such as poor diet, lack of exercise, thyroid issues, and other illnesses that can often contribute to disordered emotions. Following this, you should ask for Christ's help to renew your commitment to him so you can glorify him as you handle your negative emotions. God will certainly bless and enable such a desire.

Feelings Sometimes Lie

You have probably already noticed that your emotions can sometimes lead you to believe things that aren't true. One of the reasons this happens is because our emotions are often linked to our desires. Just as our feelings have been affected by sin, our desires are also influenced by sin.

We were created to desire God and long to glorify him. The psalmist expresses the desire like this, "As the deer pants for streams of water, so my soul pants for you, O God" (Psalm 42:1). Because of sin, however, our desires are often warped and twisted. Rather than wanting to glorify God, far too often we want to pursue desires that focus on ourselves. We want to be respected, or we want to be in control; we want to be accepted or we want to live comfortable lives without stress or pressure.

These desires and others become the grid through which we interpret what happens to us, and these interpretations powerfully influence our emotions.

Consider Donna, Kathy, and Mei. If Donna longs to be accepted, this will influence her interpretation of how others respond to her. Donna may walk into social situations on high alert for any nuance that she is being accepted or rejected. If no one at church moves toward her immediately (perhaps because her defensiveness causes her to appear unapproachable), Donna may interpret others' lack of initiative as cliquishness and feel like an outsider, lonely and isolated. In this hypothetical situation, Donna feels lonely and isolated because her desires have influenced her interpretation of the situation.

Think how her experience might have been different if Donna longed to see others enjoy deep relationships. If this was Donna's desire, when she saw others talking and laughing with each other, her response might have been pleasure. She may have concluded that this church was a place where warm relationships could be developed, and she may have approached others, assuming she also would be welcomed and included. Or she may have seen someone standing alone, looking isolated, and moved toward them to offer fellowship.

Desires can also influence Kathy's response to her son's temper tantrum. If Kathy longs for respect, she will likely view her four-year-old's tantrum through this grid. The result of her son's childish behavior will stir up emotions of embarrassment and perhaps frustration with her son because he created the circumstances that caused her embarrassment. Kathy's emotions have been influenced by her desires—what she believes she needs.

However, if Kathy's strongest desire for her son is that he come to know the grace of Christ and his power to help him in difficult situations, her response to this event might lead her to compassion and grief for her son. Her emotions may respond differently because her desires are different.

Finally, if Mei desires a life without pressure or stress, she will be influenced to interpret her professor's evaluation of her thesis as demoralizing, rather than as an invigorating challenge and an aid to get better.

In each of these examples, Donna, Kathy, and Mei experienced powerful emotions based on their interpretation of their situation—an interpretation they believed to be the truth. Their interpretation was influenced by what they believed they needed—acceptance, respect, or relief from stress. They may be completely off in their interpretation because they don't see their situation according to the truth that comes from God or they want something they are convinced they need when God may be giving them something different.

Christ can begin to change our desires. This may or may not result in more immediate positive emotions (remember Christ experienced sorrow to such an extent that he was described as a man of sorrows), but there can be an underlying joy that sustains us. On the cross, Christ despised the shame and looked instead to the joy set before him (Hebrews 12:1–2). James tells us we can consider trials pure joy because if we persevere we can become people who look like

Christ, people who are mature and complete, lacking nothing (James 1:2–4).

When we notice that our desire for God has been replaced with our own desires, we can ask for forgiveness—we can tell Jesus all about what we want and how sorry we are that we are living for ourselves instead of him. We can ask for the Spirit to give us new desires so that we grow in desiring nothing on earth but Christ and his kingdom. We can ask Jesus, through his Spirit, to supply us with what we truly need (a growing love for God and people), and to give us the strength to turn from our own desires. As we do so we can begin to experience emotional changes. Our emotions can begin to accurately reflect the emotions of our Creator, and our feelings won't lead us to believe things that aren't true. Positive emotions can be brilliant reflections of enjoying God, and redeemed negative emotions can be catalysts to help us recalibrate our desires and experience greater joy.

Make Your Feelings Work for You

As we noted earlier, feelings are part of God's good design for us. God created us with feelings, and it would be a mistake to conclude that feelings are bad. Being *enslaved* to feelings is bad. However, feelings make great servants. Let's consider some ways feelings can serve us.

Feelings can alert us to desires gone wrong.

Feelings can serve as warning signals that a desire or idol has displaced Jesus as the one you want to worship. While our desires are not always wrong in and of themselves, our emotional responses and the actions they prompt when those desires aren't met can be good indicators that we have been deceived into believing that our desires will bring more satisfaction than a relationship with Christ. Our feelings can be helpful servants if we use them as we would the red engine light that comes on to indicate a problem with an automobile engine. The light warns us there is a problem that should be addressed immediately. Feelings can serve the same purpose, alerting us to a desire or idol that needs to be addressed immediately. This does not mean that all feelings, even strong ones, are motivated by wrong desires and indicate idolatry, but sometimes even appropriate emotional responses such as anger at injustice or sadness over a loss can go in the wrong direction when our desires shift away from God's desires. It is a good idea to keep an eye on the "engine light."

For example, Kathy desires that her son obey her. That is a good desire—and God has given her the task of making sure he does learn to obey. But when he disobeys Kathy in the store, she feels embarrassment and anger. She loses control and yells at him. What might be better? Kathy could use her feelings of anger and embarrassment to alert her to the fact that what she wants in that moment is ruling her life, instead of what God wants. She is being ruled by her fear of others' opinions about her parenting and perhaps also anger that she is not getting what she wants (an obedient child). She can breathe a quick prayer asking Jesus for help, take a deep breath, and remember what is true—that God is in charge of her and her son and his Spirit is present to help them both. Then she can quietly remind her son how he needs to act and apply the appropriate consequences. She might even be able to have a conversation with him about his feelings and how he doesn't need to be ruled by them.

How about you? What feelings tend to overwhelm you? Think now about what desires might be underlying those feelings? Next time you are in the grip of negative emotions, ask Jesus, through his Spirit, to help you understand what might be ruling your heart instead of love for God and people. Ask your faithful Savior to help you turn toward him in your time of need.

Feelings can help us develop a greater appreciation for what Christ suffered in our place.

People who have been hurt badly and undergone great suffering are often equipped to have a deeper appreciation for the suffering that Christ endured for us. Think about a time in your life during which you suffered deeply. Do you remember what the feelings were like? As you remember the emotional pain of that time, does it help you better understand what Christ experienced?

He was despised and rejected by men, a man of sorrows, and familiar with suffering. Like one from whom men hide their faces he was despised, and we esteemed him not. Surely he took up our infirmities and carried our sorrows, yet we considered him stricken by God, smitten by him, and afflicted. But he was pierced for our transgressions, he was crushed for our iniquities; the punishment that brought us peace was upon him, and by his wounds we are healed. (Isaiah 53:3–5)

The things Christ suffered for us take on new significance when the horror and suffering of the cross are heightened by our feelings. As a result, our gratitude for and joy in our Savior can be exponentially increased.

Bad feelings can have eternal benefit if we use them to turn our hearts toward God. The bad feelings can help us to

- cultivate gratitude for the suffering of Christ on our behalf.
- hate sin.
- long for heaven.
- loosen our grip on what is only temporary.
- make us more concerned about where others will spend eternity.
- identify with others in their suffering.

In this way we follow Christ in his suffering and participate in his redemption by using what could have been only bad to produce something good.

Feelings allow us to express joy and gladness with passion.

James 5:13 encourages us to use good feelings to bring glory to Christ. In this verse we're told, "Is anyone happy? Let him sing songs of praise." God gives good things to enjoy (1 Timothy 6:17) and good feelings would certainly fall in that category. Think of the good feelings associated with romantic love in marriage, the birth of a son or daughter, the first flowers of spring, the salvation decision of a family member, the completion of a significant project, a hard won victory over a sinful habit, the joy of being an heir with Christ. God was good in creating us with feelings.

Good feelings are certainly a blessing, but even they should be our servants, not our masters. We should use them to add passion to our praise of God and to increase our love and devotion to him. We should use good feelings to help us eagerly pursue being like Christ and to help us take new steps of growth.

Notice how Israel used their good feelings to praise the Lord after they were liberated from being slaves to the Egyptians.

> Then Moses and the Israelites sang this song
> to the LORD:
>> "I will sing to the LORD,
>> for he is highly exalted.
>> The horse and its rider
>> he has hurled into the sea.
>> The LORD is my strength and my song;
>> he has become my salvation.
>> He is my God, and I will praise him,
>> my father's God, and I will exalt him. . . .
>> The LORD will reign for ever and ever."
>> (Exodus 15:1–2, 18)[4]

Hannah expressed her feelings of thankfulness for a child in 1 Samuel 2 by praising God. David was so happy he expressed his feelings in dancing to the Lord

(2 Samuel 6:14). When Mary learned she was to be the mother of Jesus, she expressed her feelings in a song of praise (Luke 1:46–55). Zacchaeus expressed his gladness for salvation by giving to the poor and making restitution to those from whom he had stolen (Luke 19:1–9). Good feelings make great servants.

Not only was God good in creating us with feelings to serve us in this life, God promises that we can look forward to good feelings forever in heaven with him. Psalm 16:11 says, "You have made known to me the path of life; you will fill me with joy in your presence, with eternal pleasures at your right hand." At that time we'll fully experience the freedom that is in Jesus. Keep going to Jesus now. Make it your ambition to desire him above all else. As you do, you'll experience less bondage to your emotions and more and more of the freedom Jesus has promised.

Endnotes

1. See, for example, Ephesians 4:30; Psalm 78:40–41; Isaiah 62:5; Isaiah 65:19; Isaiah 16; Psalm 60:6; John 3:16.

2. Sinclair Ferguson, *Children of the Living God* (Edinburgh; Carlisle, PA: The Banner of Truth Trust, 1989), 35.

3. For a fuller discussion of how Christ lifts our shame, see Edward T. Welch, *Shame Interrupted: How God Lifts the Pain of Worthlessness and Rejection* (Greensboro, NC: New Growth Press, 2012).

4. Note: Only a small portion of Israel's response is included here. To see the full expression of Israel's feelings, read all of Exodus 15.